KINSLEY THORLEY

NEVER LOSE A CUSTOMER AGAIN

The Ultimate Guide on How To Get and Keep Your Customers, Learn the Essentials and Useful Tips on How to Effectively Retain Your Customers

Descrierea CIP a Bibliotecii Naționale a României
KINSLEY THORLEY
    NEVER LOSE A CUSTOMER AGAIN. The Ultimate Guide on How To Get and Keep Your Customers, Learn the Essentials and Useful Tips on How to Effectively Retain Your Customers / Kinsley Thorley – Bucharest: Editura My Ebook, 2021
    ISBN

KINSLEY THORLEY

NEVER LOSE A CUSTOMER AGAIN
The Ultimate Guide on How To Get and Keep Your Customers, Learn the Essentials and Useful Tips on How to Effectively Retain Your Customers

My Ebook Publishing House
Bucharest, 2021

TABLE OF CONTENTS

Introduction 7

Chapter 1 - Customer Retention 11
Seven Infallible Strategies for Customer Retention 12

Chapter 2 - Member Retention 27
Seven specific ways to retain members on your membership website 29

Chapter 3 - List Retention 37
Five things you can do to maintain your list and retain list members 38

Conclusion 43

INTRODUCTION

The results of an online loyalty study published in Harvard Business Review reveal that for the typical business, a five-percent increase in customer retention translates to anywhere between a 25 and 95 percent increase in profits. That's the power of customer retention for you!

But you don't need Harvard Business Review to tell you that, do you? As the engaged owner of an online business, you are already aware how vital *and* critical customer retention is for business sustainability and profitability.

You may have witnessed first hand that customers you have retained successfully over the years: visit your website, blog, and e-commerce platform more often; shop at your online store more frequently; spend more than the average buyer during each purchase; and stay with you during relatively adverse times, such as increased prices or customer services glitches, as well.

They are your most loyal customers who patronize you, are more accepting of your business (ready to try new products or purchase costlier items), and more forgiving of your faults (ready to give you a second chance in case of faulty product or service delivery).

Far ahead of other happy customers, these people are your brand advocates, evangelists if you will, who promote your business to friends and family. There is significant dollar value to each of these advantages loyal customers provide you.

For instance:

A two percent increase in customer retention will roughly have the same effect as a 10percent reduction in selling price. Source: "Leading on the Edge of Chaos", Emmet Murphy & Mark Murphy.

Retaining customers lowers your total customer acquisition costs and is in fact, six to seven times cheaper than acquiring a new customer. Source: Bain & Company

Your chances of selling to an existing customer is anywhere between 60 and 70 percent, whereas that of selling to a newly-acquired customer is typically between five and 20 percent. **Source: Marketing Metrics**

Retained customers (loyal customers) are more profitable – they have a higher lifetime value; make more purchases; spend more per purchase; are more accepting of price increases; are more likely to show similar loyalty for other products and services you launch; bring more business to you by referring more people. **Source: "The Value of Online Customer Loyalty", Bain & Company**

Think that's good? Wait until you hear more!

Not only are retained customers more loyal and profitable but so are the referred customers they bring to you. Another Harvard Business Review study found that new customers acquired through customer referrals generate more revenue at lower costs.

Again, this makes sense in the practical world as well. Even without the presence of a journal review, you may have witnessed how referred customers tend to treat you almost as good as the loyal customers who referred them to you. They come to you with zero customer acquisition cost, and spend nearly as much as the frequently-shopping loyal customers you have.

And it's not just about customer retention. Retention of any sort, whether it is that of your employees; the members of your membership website; or the subscribers of your email-marketing list – has specific monetary advantages seconded by virtually nothing else.

You will agree therefore, that when it comes to customer retention, the question is not so much 'why' it is more about 'how'.

So without further ado, let's get to the answer. This e-book will be your guide in retaining leads, customers, subscribers, and members. Included over the course of three chapters are diverse tips, tricks, and strategies to help you enjoy stellar success in terms of retention.

CHAPTER 1

CUSTOMER RETENTION

The success of your customer retention strategies will depend heavily upon three key factors, which are essentially the pillars of stellar customer retention. These include your ability to:

- Make (and keep) customers happy
- Reduce customer effort
- Delivery quality customer service; first time, every time

Consequently, all strategies created to address one or more of the factors listed above, will contribute effectively towards customer retention.

Depending upon the needs of your business in particular, you can create strategies focusing on any one (again, or more) of these factors and drive retention through the roof.

Seven Infallible Strategies for Customer Retention

Listed below are seven of the simplest, most pertinent steps that will help you get started:

Step #1: Recognize customers as nothing short of valuable assets

…And treat them such!

One of the biggest determinants of loyalty is the buying experience a customer has when on your e-commerce platform. Research by McKinsey reveals that a whopping 70 percent of buying experiences are a function of how customers feel they are being treated; which is why it is important for you to clarify what customers truly 'mean' to your business and consequently, how they should be treated, from the get go.

This will ensure no customer is ever treated like a transaction, instead of being treated as a valued asset, and is your first step towards improving retention.

The second step is to make and keep customers happy through timely delivery of exceptional customer service.

Here are a few suggestions:

- **Prioritize service**

Contrary to what traditional media will have you believe, product or price are *not* the key reasons of churn. It's customer service or service delivery.

The Accenture Global Customer Satisfaction Report (2008) reveals that "overall poor quality of customer service" is the main reason for customer attrition. Results of a Bain & Company report reveal that service-related problems increase the likelihood of customer attrition four times as much as product- or price-related problems.

There exists a body of other independent researchers that conclude the same – more customers leave you because they don't like your service, than when they don't like your products or prices.

The need to prioritize service delivery and customer service is easy to see now, isn't it? Communicate the need internally within your organization; educate customer-facing staff in the mantras of great customer service; and set up systems to monitor the service delivered by your personnel.

- **Get proactive**

Proactive customer service is the next-generation of customer service philosophies. Compared to its traditional counterpart, which involves fire-fighting problems as they occur; proactive customer service is anticipatory in nature and involves nipping problems in the bud even before they occur.

Delivering proactive customer service can be as simple as calling a customer after they have received the product, and inquiring whether or not everything was okay.

It can be as not-so-simple as texting customers about an expected delay in shipment or advising them about a due payment weeks in advance. It can also be as complex as informing customers about an expected drop in prices of the product they recently purchased, sometime in the near future and advising them on their next steps. Amazon for instance, offers a best-in-industry price-drop refund that allows customers to request reimbursement on the difference if prices drop within a week of purchase.

What anticipatory customer service means for your staff will depend upon the details of your business. However, it helps to remember that any support extended to the customer from your side, *before* the customer comes asking for it, is proactive service and will help you boost loyalty.

- **Get personal**

Gone are the days when you could address someone as "Dear customer" and still be on their good books. The plethora of customer relationship management tools have made it possible for businesses to treat every single one of their customers with personalization and customization.

Best-practices in customer service personalization include using names in all brand communications (written or verbal), using the right words to show empathy, and providing relevant (customized) solutions to customer problems. Phrases like "I don't know, but I will find out for you.", "I would be happy to help you with this.", "I can understand, I would be frustrated too.", and "Thank you miss Jane, is there anything else I can help you with?" show you care about the experience of customers and makes them happy.

Above everything else, be sure to resolve customer problems as soon as possible, and as effectively as possible. The White House Office of Consumer Affair reveals that satisfied customers who have had their issues resolved and are happy with it, share their experience with about four to six people, spreading good word about your business in the process.

- **Get delightful**

One of the most sure-fire ways to unleash retentiveness of your current customer base is to aim to delight (and not just satisfy) customers through customer service.

Proactive services and personalized, empathetic responses will help you make and keep customers happy. However, to delight them you will have to up the ante with gifts and surprises that show reciprocity.

Reciprocity, which is the act of doing something good for someone in response to the good they do or have done for you, is touted by many to be the number one factor that builds loyalty.

Make the best use of it by providing sweet surprises to your customers and delighting them time and again. You may send a free gift, a special loyalty discount, and other special offers to show appreciation for their loyalty.

Do not try to sell anything with these gifts and put no terms or conditions of use to your loyalty gift cards. Instead, allow complete freedom of use to customers for that truly delightful experience. This way customers will remember you even when faced by competition.

Step #2: Build a relationship that's larger than your business

Sure, sales of your products or services are the key to staying afloat. However, they should not be your only concern. Sales in fact are sometimes a funny thing - they sometimes come to you when you stop chasing them.

So what should you do instead? Focus on building a strong, profitable relationship with your customers. A relationship that is larger than your business.

One of the easiest ways to cement relationships with customers is to care about shared values.

Stand up for something – a social cause, a deep-rooted value, an operational philosophy – that can strike a chord with your customers and will boost loyalty among like-minded customers.

No we are not kidding! Results of a Corporate Executive Board study found that 64 percent of the 7,000 U.S. customers who cited having a "strong bond" with a brand listed *shared values* as the number one reason! This is because consumers are increasingly getting socially conscious and they want their companies to be so too.

Taking a public stand on social issues will also help you deliver your corporate social responsibility beliefs, boosting loyalty further.

The 2013 Cone Communications Social Impact Study found that 80 percent of American consumers are likely to switch from non-conscious brands to socially-conscious brands provided comparable quality and affordability. In addition, the 2014 Nielsen Doing Well by Doing Good study reveals that 42 percent customers from North America said they would be okay paying extra for products and services that came from companies creating positive social and/or environmental impact.

Step #3: Stay in touch constantly

Through regular communication, you will be able to create and reach a state of top-of-mind awareness (TOMA) among your target market segment, which will not just boost retention but also prevent attrition.

TOMA is when customers think of your brand or platform without advertisement. It's when they think about your company first, before the name of your competitors comes to their mind.

The good news is, much of top-of-mind awareness is related with brand awareness and recall, both of which can be maximized through regular communication.

- Start by creating social media platforms (if you don't have them already). You want to have a company page on the 'big three' of social media (Facebook, Twitter, & Google Plus) as well as the professional networking giant LinkedIn and the photo-sharing websites (either) Pinterest or Instagram.
- Link these social profiles with your business website or e-commerce platform. Set up automatic sharing of content through all channels to boost content visibility. There are a host of social media marketing tools (listed below) that will help you automate this task and more.
- Create an editorial calendar to ensure you are churning out enough fresh content on a regular basis. Use tools such as Post Planner, Beatrix, Feedly, Scoop.it, and Storify to name a few, to automatically find and share relevant content; Buffer and its extension BulkBuffer to schedule mass posts according to your editorial calendar; Bundle Post for automatic sourcing and sharing of popular, authoritative tweets from your industry and so on.

With a little research you will find that it may not even be necessary to use different tools for different tasks. Apps such as Feedly and Scoop.it can perform all tasks from content curation, long and short-term scheduling, multi-channel sharing, and even analytics.

- Next, shift your attention to blogging – one of the most evergreen and effective content marketing strategies since the beginning of online marketing. You want to keep your blog posts either educational or entertaining but never 'salesy'. A blogging best-practice is to add value to readers' lives by sharing content they will find helpful. For instance, if you sell software products, your posts can talk about the do's and don'ts of purchasing software products online, the pitfalls online purchasers should be wary of, so on and so forth. Be sure to invite readers to share their two cents by leaving you comments.

- Take blogging to the next level by inviting noted industry bloggers, the 'influencers' to make guest posts on your blog. This will add further credibility and boost reputation among readers. Further, be sure to find and utilize any opportunities of guest blogging on authoritative websites. This will expose you to the already loyal readers of the blog on which you are posting as a guest, give you new followers, and also establish you as a much sought after thought leader.

There are a host of tools, technologies, and services to make this easy for you. One of the best ways to go would be to hire one or more content writers. If you cannot afford to have a full-time writer in house, you can opt for freelance content writers from websites such as Elance, Freelancer, Upwork, People per Hour, and Freelance Writing Gigs to name a few.

There's a third option as well. If you already have a small content team at hand, you can make them more effective by using the content marketing tools and technologies of today. For instance, your team can improve readership of blog posts by using the King Sumo application to improve blog headlines. The application is a WordPress plugin that lets you create up to 10 alternative titles for your blog posts and check in real time, which is the best performing headline to be used for the final post. Here's a quick list of 18 nifty tools you can use to improve content writing, increase content frequency and speed, boost communications, and raise top- of-mind awareness for increased retention and reduced attrition.

Step #4: Talk to the ones that got away

Find out what triggered attrition in the customers that chose to leave you for competitors.

One easy way would be to invite customers to fill-up a quick feedback form as they uninstall your app, or unsubscribe from your email marketing and newsletters.

Other ways to get in touch with customers who seemed to have churned is to simply pick up the phone and ask them what put them off. This works especially well for small businesses, where you can easily point out who your most ideal customers are and get in touch with them personally. Remember, you don't want all customers back, only the ones who had been ideal customers before something put them off and they turned to a competitor.

Compared to the 60 to 70 percent chance you have of re-selling to a current customer, there is a 20 to 40 percent chance of selling to an ex-customer by winning them back. And winning back is a three-step procedure. After you have reviewed their purchase history with you and decided that you do want them back:

1. Get in touch with them *promptly* to find out what went wrong. You may use mail or telephone, depending on what has been the preferred medium of communication used by the deferred customer in the past.

2. Take responsibility for what went wrong, while communicating clearly what you plan to do in order to ensure the same problem does not occur again.

3. Present a new offer to the customer, depending upon their complaint. Or simply ask them if you could keep sending them industry-specific information and offers as you did before. The idea at this stage is to have the lost customer open at least one channel of communication between themselves and your business.

Once they have agreed to it, you can slowly push relevant, informative, and high-value non- salesy content to them. Be sure to send any offers and discounts you are hosting their way, and before long, they will be ready to make their first purchase as a won-back customer.

Step #5: Talk to the ones that chose to stay

This is an easy one. Invite the most loyal of your customers to participate in a small survey to help you improve your products and services.

Position these surveys or feedback forms to follow typical 'gain points' in their purchase cycle (such as when a successful delivery has been made, or when they have successfully used a discount coupon for a purchase). The idea is to find out what product/service, service delivery, and customer service factors appeals the most to your loyal customers. You can also invite customers in for a detailed feedback. But you will need to include small rewards to encourage participation in these long-form surveys or feedback.

Use what you learn from these surveys to boost your product/service quality, customer service delivery, and general customer experience. Focus on what the customers have pointed out as positive. And aim to minimize what customers pointed out as negative (from strategy #4).

Step #6: Invest in key areas that make customers' lives easy

Start with the areas where you are weak.

Your customers may have pointed these areas out, or you may have found them out through test runs conducted on-site. If unsure, you may even get in touch with your customer service personnel to list and prioritize the most common complaints or problems customers share with them.

You will find that the majority of these areas will fall into one or more of the following categories – order fulfillment (for speedy dispatch and delivery), customer service (for timely customer support and complaint resolution), website or e-commerce platform functionality (for ease of product search, research, and order placement), or pricing (for more competitive prices or higher affordability).

The key to success here is prioritizing the improvement initiatives because chances are, you will not be able to undertake all of them at the same time.

A good place to start is to check which single area produces the largest number of problems or complaints. Another way to start is to check which single improvement will result in remarkable customer experience improvement. Updating your website to improve page-load times, optimize navigation, increase search precision, and/or to add additional functionality will have a lasting impact on the overall shopping experience of your customers, thereby boosting loyalty. You could for instance, invest in an advanced, state-of-the-art website that eliminates complexity for users through the use of diverse functionality like multiple 'filters' for search; notification choices for out-of-stock products; enhanced visibility of product information; and the like.

Another great investment will be a system for stellar email marketing. Despite being one of the oldest forms of digital marketing, email marketing *is* one of the most profitable forms of inbound marketing in terms of return on investment. Use tools such as Mail Chimp, Target Hero, and Campaigner to automate the process while getting the most out of your investment on email marketing.

Step #7: Remember to reward loyalty

…And implementing a customer loyalty program is one of the best ways there is to reward loyalty.

The simplest of loyalty programs, which include rewards on second purchases or on reaching a set dollar figure, are surprisingly effective in making your customers feel special and in making them stick to your brand.

Shopify has a great app Klaviyo that keeps track of the spends of individual customers and mails reward coupons to them automatically when they have crossed a landmark.

You can also invest in more comprehensive loyalty programs, such as those that offer rewards for completing tasks like creating an account or referring a friend. Use tools such as Loyalty Lion and SLoyalty to easily set up these loyalty programs, implement, and manage them.

And finally, be sure to keep monitoring and measuring customer satisfaction as well as monthly churn and retention. This will help you see which strategies are working for you and which aren't. Focus on the customer retention strategies that are working and eliminate or optimize the ones that aren't able to reach high levels of retention within a relatively short span of time.

CHAPTER 2

MEMBER RETENTION

Much like customer retention, membership retention stands upon the three pillars of making and keeping members happy, reducing their efforts, and delivering quality service to them time and again.

It is a good idea therefore, to start your member retention efforts in the same manner as you would start a customer retention program.

Include the seven steps of:

1. Assigning top priority to members and ensuring they are treated as assets and not as transactions; prioritizing customer support & service; making communications highly personable; and aiming to go beyond 'satisfaction' with *delight.*

2. Investing in long-term, value-added relationship building which covers more than just the product or service your membership website caters to.

3. Staying in constant touch through quality content published timely and on multiple channels. Here, you can easily integrate your membership site to social media sites for improved communication.

4. Getting in touch with former members who canceled their membership or failed to renew it after the end of membership period; to uncover the reasons that contributed to their churning.

5. Getting in touch with current members who happen to be your most loyal or most long- standing members, and find out the key qualities of your membership site they appreciate the most.

6. Investing in building a great, feature-packed, albeit easy-to-use membership website to reduce member effort. Investing in other high-quality, high-value technologies such as one-step reminder or notification integration; efficient email marketing and newsletter integration; and so on to boost site usability.

7. Rewarding the most loyal members (the most longtime members, or relatively newer members who show high

engagement and loyalty) with appropriate rewards and tokens of appreciation.

It is worth noting that while the basics of retention (whether of customers, members, or mailing list) remain same, the specifics change with each section of people you are trying to retain.

Thus, the seven steps briefed above (which you may remember from the previous chapter) are to be taken as a framework for your member retention initiatives.

Seven specific ways to retain members on your membership website

Listed below are six super effective yet simple and cost-effective tips to help you customize the framework from above according to the nature of your membership website.

1. Understand the reasons why people (may) abandon *your* membership site

Some of the most common reasons why people abandon memberships are:
- Poor leadership
- Poor communication between members
- Complacency or apathy from some members

- Lack of proper on-boarding or orientation at the beginning
- Inadequate membership activities/opportunities
- Lack of sufficient participation/involvement from members
- Lack of sufficient membership projects

…to name a few.

You must find out which it is for the members of your website or community and then act quickly to address the reason at source.

Surveying relatively new members (say those that have been with you for three or four weeks) about what they would like done differently on the site or community is a good way to get started. Requesting a quick feedback from former members who have terminated their membership or not renewed it is another way to go about it.

There may be other opportunities as well, when you will find it easy to talk to members or former members about the reasons why they may leave or have left you. Understanding these reasons and acting upon them is the first step towards making your membership more alluring and welcoming for current and prospective members.

2. Start thinking retention from the get go

You want to start 'wooing' members into long-term membership right from the time they join you.

The trick is to keep this courtship action-based, and not verbal. What does that mean you ask? It's quite simple really. Instead of communicating how much you want members to stay long term, show them how great it would be for them if they stayed long term

Your first step will be to nail new-member induction with an educational, meaningful, and impressive orientation. Next, assign the new member to a loyal member you have had over the years, for guidance and general mentoring wherever required.

Ensure you establish at least four additional contacts (contacts that are above and below the normal) with a new member during the first year of their membership and shower them with personal attention.

On a strategic level, you want to create yearly, quarterly, or monthly retention goals and undertake activities to meet your goals. For instance, once you decide upon a monthly retention rate, you will be able to chalk out a plan to create resources and activities for members that boost engagement and prevent churn.

In addition, you want to establish an 'involvement committee' that serves the purpose of boosting participation and therefore engagement among members. Give your involvement committee the freedom to brainstorm participation and engagement strategies and to act upon them.

3. Focus on making networking easy for members

Networking is one of the primary reasons members have for joining online websites and communities within their industry. This is why you want to ensure you make networking easy for members so that the membership feels worthwhile to them.

One easy way to do so is to conduct events focused on networking. You can invite members of your membership website or community for a physical meeting in the real world for example.

If your membership spans people across diverse geographical locations, co-ordinate with the most loyal members of a particular location to take the responsibility for organizing and hosting such an event.

You can also conduct meetings via video conferencing over Skype or Google Hangouts.

Then there is the option to conduct focus groups via telephone. The point is, there are several opportunities for owners of membership websites to organize, simplify, and promote networking and you must leverage these opportunities to do just that.

Also be sure to include valuable networking-related content in your articles, blog posts, email marketing newsletters and other content pieces you create for members, to make networking easy for them. You could for instance, create a checklist or a detailed article about the ways and means with which members can make the most of these networking opportunities.

4. Keep meaningful activities flowing

Activities are the backbone of engagement when it comes to membership retention. And it is easy to see why you want your activities to be meaningful. Only meaningful activities can add value to members and make them *want* to stay.

While the exact nature and number of activities you host will vary from industry to industry, niche to niche, and even website to website; you want to keep most of these activities related to – 1) boosting participation among members, 2) helping members find multiple networking opportunities and making the most of them, and 3) educating members in topics related directly to the industry or niche to which your membership website belongs.

5. Be proactive about membership renewals

Pro-activity in terms of membership renewals is a natural extension of thinking about retention from the get go.

You want to create effective renewal campaigns that drive current members towards early renewal. Start by segmenting customers into different groups based upon the reason of their joining. Send targeted renewal mails to them, pointing out how membership benefited them over the last year, and how it will benefit them the coming year.

You may also use jeopardy marketing tactics (pointing what a current member stands to lose by failing to renew membership) as well, instead of pointing out only what they have gained or what they stand to gain in the future. Tactics such as early-renewal incentives and renewal lotteries will work equally effectively.

For instance, you may offer an incentive such as an extended renewal period or a free gift to members who renew their membership by a certain date.

A lottery would involve encouraging people to renew membership before a certain date to gain entry into the lottery/contest.

Other forms of positive reinforcement include sharing testimonials and real-life experiences of members who have transformed the way they live, work, or play because of your membership site.

6. Reward loyalty

As always, you have got to reward loyalty. Always be on the lookout for opportunities to recognize what a member is doing for you.

Recognition can come in the form of certifications or plaques wording out the contribution of the member. When it comes to rewards, use non-monitory rewards such as free upgrades to premium services to create a sense of goodwill and delight among loyal members.

Discounts and freebies work just as good in making loyal members feel special about being a part of your community, and boosts loyalty further.

7. Compare with and stay abreast of competition

And finally, be sure you are not outbid by your competitors.

Aim to provide comparable, if not superior benefits at competitive rates. Ideally, you should try to do either something better or something completely different than your competition. This will set you apart and help in not only retention but also acquisition of members.

So there you go, these are the seven basic ways in which you can boost member retention for your membership website.

The best thing about these tips is that you can use them for virtually any type of membership site or community, including your Facebook fan page and LinkedIn groups.

CHAPTER 3

LIST RETENTION

Email marketing is one of the oldest channels of digital marketing. It is also one of the most profitable. According to the Email Marketing Industry Census (2014) published by *E-Consultancy* in association with *Adestra*, email marketing revenue witnessed a 28 percent hike in the 12 months from March 2013 to March 2014. And if history is any reliable indicator, email marketing has always been a high-return, high-revenue tactic for marketers.

68 percent of the participating organizations of the E-Consultancy study rated email as 'excellent' or 'good' in terms of marketing return-on-investment, making email marketing *the* best channel in terms of ROI.

However, this strategy is of little help when your list (of email-marketing subscribers) is constantly shrinking.

Listed below are five tips to help you keep members of your email marketing list happy and to prevent them from unsubscribing.

Five things you can do to maintain your list and retain list members

As was the case with customer retention and member retention, the pillars of list retention are happiness; ease or effortlessness; and delightful services for the email marketing subscribers on your list. Depending upon the industry or niche you serve, you want to ensure quality, value-added service delivery.

So whether you are sending emails to inform list members of new products/services they may be interested in, upcoming discounts, season specials and so on; or it is sending educational or informative content via emails and newsletters; you want all emails to contribute infallibly towards making list members' (personal or professional) life easier, better, or happier.

Content is the backbone of email marketing success and must be treated as such.

Listed below are five specific things you can do in this regard:

1. **Quit selling all the time**

Nothing disinterests list members quite as much as self-serving emails from your side.

Limit sales-focused mails to not more than one a week, unless you have special discounts, offers, or seasonal sales going on, about which members must be informed promptly. Focus on member education and engagement in other emails.

2. **Quit sending all the time**

Did you know that there is such a thing called 'email inbox fatigue'? Because there is.

Sending mails too often can overwhelm list members and turn them sour sooner than you think. Decide upon a frequency that works the best for you and stick to it. You should also try list segmentation to avoid this problem of over-sending.

Segment your subscribers according to their position and preferences so that you are not sending out tons of emails to everyone in your list. This just dilutes the effect of your content and pushes subscribers who find the content irrelevant towards hitting that unsubscribe button.

If you use email-marketing solutions from popular vendors such as Mail Chimp, you will be able to segment customers easy and put them into even smaller groups to which you can send highly specific content.

3. Offer personalization of content

Allow members to personalize their email communications with you by indicating their preferences in terms of the content and frequency of mails they receive.

You can create interest groups and allow list members to sort themselves into group(s) of their choice.

A good idea is to include a link to update preferences in all mails. This will allow fatigued or unsatisfied members to change their preferences or to move themselves to a more suitable interest group, instead of unsubscribing completely.

Speaking of content, you want to ensure you content is both relevant and useful to members because as you may know by now, it is the backbone of email marketing and therefore, the fundamental determinant of email marketing success for your organization.

4. Display a permission reminder and unsubscribe link in all mails

A permission reminder tells list members why they are receiving mails from you. They are editable pieces of content included in the footer of typical emails and are an anti-spam requirement aswell.

An unsubscribe link is another anti-spam requirement. It also displays good faith on your part by reassuring members they are in control of the email marketing relationship and can walk out of it when they want.

5. Target members who seem to be falling out of love

You may have members who have unsubscribed to your email marketing communications 'mentally' – members who are still subscribed to you but do not respond to mails.

They may delete the mails without opening and leave them unopened and unread in their inbox. You want to stop pushing marketing messages to them and send them down the path of re-engagement instead.

Make the experience positive for them by demonstrating you understand something is not quite right and that you want them to tell you want they want (by updating preferences) to make it work.

Tailor your content for re-engagement instead of sales or customer education at this point to actively help members find interest in membership again.

Bonus tip: *Proactively de-clutter your list of inactive/unresponsive list members and of customers who delete your mails or have unsubscribed already.*

This will help you narrow your focus on current members of the list/interest group so you will have a deeper insight into the kind of content that works best with them. This will improve targeting for you, boosting engagement and subsequently retention.

CONCLUSION

Retention – whether of leads, prospects and customers, or of site members and email subscribers is all about keeping the people in question happy and helping them see clear value in being a stakeholder of your business.

Your strategies should focus on making things easy for them by eliminating any unnecessary friction and by reducing the total effort it may take a customer or member or subscriber to find what they desire or need.

And you should prioritize service delivery, making it as stellar and delightful as possible because ultimately it's how you serve customers or members that matters the most.

Given the high degree of competitiveness pertinent in today's business world, products or service solutions are already comparable. It's the customer support, service, and quality of service delivery that differentiates a great business from an average one.

Remember to tweak individual strategies depending upon the segment of customers you are targeting. And use the host of tips provided in the e-book to create a culture of retention in every business function at your organization – from selling to customers or website members to marketing to leads, prospects, email marketing subscribers, and more.

www.ingramcontent.com/pod-product-compliance
Ingram Content Group UK Ltd.
Pitfield, Milton Keynes, MK11 3LW, UK
UKHW022213230426
12048UKWH00016BA/821